Lost Ancient Technology Of Peru And Bolivia: Volume 2

Authored By Brien Foerster

Close up of some of the artifacts

Located on the Bolivian shore of Lake Titicaca and close to the Peru/Bolivia border is the small village of Santiago de Ojje, far off the tourist route. Like many of the obscure ancient sites in Peru and Bolivia, I stumbled upon photos of these ruins while searching through

1

internet photos. Finding the location on a map is one thing, and finding the actual location is another matter. Luckily, a client of ours, Diana showed interest in visiting the site, along with our friend Antonio Portugal, who is very well known Bolivian author and lives in La Paz. As we were in the Lake Titicaca area anyway, we set off one morning with our driver/friend Eduardo and got quite close to the location, within a 10 minute drive when Eduardo's van suddenly stopped working. With a friendly shrug of his shoulders Eduardo found us a local taxi to take us the rest of the way as he figured out what was wrong with his vehicle.

Megalithic stones protruding from the dirt

The taxi driver was confident that he knew the specific location we were looking for, but just to make sure I kept my eyes focused on the left side of the car. He sped along quite fast and suddenly a shaped stone, weighing at least one ton appeared close to the left side of the road. I told him to stop, which he did abruptly, not knowing that the stone was even there. The stone was very square in shape and clearly not a natural formation, so I kept walking towards the lake, which was relatively close, and stumbled across the complex.

The main stone of interest is this one with a coiled snake

Only one of the perimeter walls of this presumed ceremonial site is to some degree intact, though very badly damaged. Whether the destructive force was by humans or a natural event is unknown, but the local villagers over the course of centuries have used the broken pieces in their own house constructions.

The author with the "snake stone"

It appears that the original structure was either square or slightly rectangular in shape, with each side being about 40 meters long. The central area is about a meter higher than the surrounding area, and the large stones made up essentially retaining walls. Where the very dense sandstone was from was not known by the local villagers we spoke with, but they did say it was not local and a study of the area proved that to be the case.

4

View of the "snake stone" and remains of the wall

The odd black streak found on the stone with the coiled snake appears to have been soot of some kind, but from a localized fire? Likely not. It could be, though repeated visits to the site will have to be conducted, that the site was struck by an ancient cataclysm, such as that referred to in my book Aftershock. That appears to be more likely than quarrying activity by local people as the large and somewhat megalithic stones show major breaks, and no signs of tool marks were seen.

The few academics that have been to the site believe that the Tiwanaku culture were responsible for creating Santiago de Ojje, but that is very unlikely. The Tiwanaku were a bronze age people and thus could not have shaped these large stones. Curiously though, the snake appears to be looking towards the Tiwanaku complex, which is southeast of the site.

Horca de Inca

Despite its name, the Horca del Inca was thought to have been built by the pre-Inca Chiripa culture in the 14th century BC as an astronomical observatory. Rituals on the winter soltice June 21 were also held here. When the Spanish came along, they supposedly destroyed some of the site in the hopes of finding gold hidden there. Noting its resemblance to a gallows and mistakenly associating it with the Inca, they gave the monument its present name.

The trilithic (three-rock) structure resembles a gallows, hence its popular name. Between the two naturally upright rocks, the Chiripa builders placed seven horizontal rock slabs in precise positions that would enable observation of the heavenly bodies. On the equinoxes, the sun can be viewed as it reflects off the rocks.

There is only one cross-piece left in position today, thanks to the Spanish, and unfortunately the rocks have been decorated with graffiti. However, the ancient site still has plenty of ambience as well as fine views of Lake Titicaca and the town of Copacabana. The Inca name for this place is Pachat'aqa.

Lake Titicaca as seen near the Horca del Inca

Sunset near the summer solstice in 2017

Basalt temple at Chucuito

The megalithic Fertility Temple also known as "Chucuito" on the edge of Lake Titicaca in Peru is special and at the same time controversial basically for a single reason: its "sexuality". Whether the upright stones are supposed to be phallic or represent magic mushrooms has caused much debate between historians for many years now.

Also known as Inka Uyo, it is a lesser known site of cut stone structures located at the site of Chucuito in Peru. It is a part of one of the two plazas that make up the site of Chucuito and according to many archaeologists, it is one of the most intriguing constructions in the Titicaca Basin, as it is an arrangement of carved stones sticking up from the earth within a walled, rectangular structure.

At first glance, Inca Uyo is a walled enclosure next to Santo Domingo that looks like a garden of giant mushrooms. But upon closer inspection, the 86 carved, mushroom-shaped stones look more like carved stone penises, some pointing up at the sky, possibly toward Inti, the Inca sun god, while others rammed into the ground, toward Pachamama, the Mother Earth goddess.

Entrance in to the main courtyard

The structures were first excavated in 1950 by Harry and Marion Tschopik, archaeologists with expertise in Peru, and who were the ones who first stated that the structures were constructed in "Inca style". The site would be further excavated by Orompelio Vidal during the 1960s, whose work mainly focused on clearing the plaza surrounding structures.

After detailed archaeological research, it has been concluded that the stones are ancient and from local quarries, although there is some debate whether the stones have been moved at some point, since the original excavation did not describe them being arranged upright into rows, as they are found today. Additionally, some experts appear to agree that many stones were collected from other locations and placed at the enclosure.

Massive basalt blocks at the entrance

As can be seen in the photo above, the enclosure is composed of two layers of walls. The one on the outside has much larger stones than that inside, and all of the stone is basalt, whether from a local source or not is unknown. The outer wall stones fit very tightly together without any mortar used, while the inner walls' stones are more roughly stacked. This likely means that the outer wall is original, made by master builders whose name and history id unknown. Whether the Inca or another culture built the inner wall is also unclear.

Three girls posing near the central altar

It is my opinion that the standing stones represent phalluses and not mushrooms, though many western observers, especially those with a fascination for psychotropic drugs insist that the "mushroom theory" is the most accurate.

Whether they are all in their original positions is doubtful, as their organization in relation to one another is rather messy. It is quite possible that originally they all faced upwards, symbolically connecting Pachamama with the sun deity Inti. Since there is a church next door on the left side in the photo above, the priests have been responsible for disrupting the interior design of the structure, and archaeologists tried to later reorganize it. It is used as a fertility temple by local people to this very day.

Detail view of the interior

The name of the small village where this ancient work is located is called Chicuito, and whether that was the name of the temple or not, and that the village was named after it is unknown. Chicuito is not an Inca name, as in from the Quechua language, but is Aymara, which is an older and more local language.

Amaru Muru near Lake Titicaca

It is not known when Aramu Muru was made and who did it, but most likely it happened before the time of the Inca. No archaeological research has been done here as far as I know.

This enormous stone portal is located in an unusual place, Hayu Marca stone forest ("City of the gods") near the shores of Lake Titicaca in Peru. Giant crests of red sandstone rise from the dry soil of the Altiplano and erosion processes have formed natural bridges, weird grottoes and natural sculptures. Often it is hard to tell whether some weird shapes have been formed by nature or by humans.

Aramu Muru is cut in the side of one such granite crest. This portal is 7 meters high and 7 meters wide, with a "T" shaped alcove in the bottom middle. The surface of the portal is worn due to too much human contact. The alcove is some 2 meters high, so one man can fit into it. In the center of alcove is a smaller depression. On the other side of the cliff in earlier times was located a tunnel, which is blocked now with stones to prevent mishaps with children. Some believe that this tunnel was going to Tiahuanaco.

Worshipping in the central niche

Legends tell that the gate was open for a while in the 16th century. Back then Spanish Conquistadors were looting the immense treasures in and slaughtering local people. In the most important Inca temple, the Coricancha, now the Church of Santo Domingo were located especially valuable relics, golden discs likely with complex calendars on them. According to the legend, these discs were given by gods to the Inca. The discs supposedly had powerful healing abilities. Two of these discs were seized by Spaniards, but the third one, the largest, disappeared without a trace.

A priest of Coricancha temple, Aramu Muru managed to escape from the deadly havoc in Cusco. He took the large golden disc with him. Aramu Muru reached the Hayu Marca hills and hid there for a while. He stumbled on Inca priests, guardians of the portal and, when the guardians saw the golden disc, there was arranged a special ritual at the gate. This secret ritual opened the giant portal and blue light was shining from it. Aramu Muru entered the portal and has never been seen again. The gate got his name some believe.

There is no similar such work as far as I know in Peru or Bolivia, and this makes it even more difficult to discern who made it and when. The red sandstone is actually relatively soft, and the surfaces not precisely flat, so it could have been achieved using quite simple hand tools.

Note the channels on each side of the central niche

Mysterious Quenuani

Almost nothing is known about Quenuani, located next to Lake Titicaca and just over the Bolivian border in Peru. It took me 5 years, after seeing a few low resolution photos of it on the internet to finally find it, but that is what perseverance is for.

One of the "benches" at Quenuani

Locating it on a map proved to be elusive, but we happened to be in the vicinity and it seemed as if we would be driving more or less right past it somewhat near the highway. Our Bolivian guide Gustavo Morales decided that we should stop at the nearby police station and ask. After 5 minutes he came and said that the police had no idea.

Sets of curved staircases at Quenuani

While Gustavo was speaking with the police chief I looked out through the right front window of the bus and saw Quenuani, about half a kilometer away. By great fortune there was a dirt road wide enough to allow the bus to take us right to the site.

Interesting curved area

This massive exposed bedrock site appears to be compressed volcanic ash, as the Andes area is largely made up of igneous formations, as well as some sandstone outcrops such as we saw at Amaru Muru. The ash is soft enough to be affected by scraping with a pocket knife, so it is not necessarily the case that lost ancient high technology was responsible in its making, though this cannot be 100 percent ruled out.

Another one of the well made staircases

What Quenuani's original function was, and who made it are unclear; most will state that the Inca produced it for which there is no evidence. Some will state that it was a quarry, but where the removed blocks are now located is unknown, others will say a performance or ceremonial space, but there is basically no data on the internet about it.

The author; note the tool marks

The so called benches do somewhat face Tiawanaku, located to the south and across the lake in Bolivia, but like Amaru Muru, I have not heard of any other ancient location that has the general appearance or configuration of what we see at Quenuani. Even local archaeologists that I have shown photos of it to simply ask where it is, because they have never heard of it. What else is located in the region that academics do not know about? Only local knowledge will tell us. Next we are off to the central highlands of Peru to explore megalithic remains between Paracas on the coast and the highland city of Ayacucho.

Main wall of the church showing different construction techniques

The Temple of Huaytara, which is the main construction of the Incas that we find in this archaeological complex, was supposedly a work of the Inca Pachacutec (Inca Yupanqui) and was built during the conquest period of the Chincha by the beginning of the 15th century AD. A century later, during the viceroyalty of Peru, and in the mission of extirpation of idolatries initiated by the Spaniards, this building would be used as a base for the construction of the Catholic church San Juan Bautista de Huaytara.

It is believed that the Inca building, under the church of San Juan Bautista, would have been destined to be a Temple of the Sun, although there are also those who think that it could have been a palace.

Regarding the architecture of the Inca temple we can say that it has the trapezoidal doors and windows typical of Inca construction. Structurally, it was made out of pink volcanic stone blocks, with a thickness of 1.65 meters and that reached a height of 3.70 meters.

Note that the upper half is adobe and the lower half solid stone

The above photo shows us that this structure was constructed in at least 3 stages. The lower half is of very dense stone blocks fitting tightly together without mortar, and the quarry is apparently some 50 kilometers away. Though I am not a geologist, the stone appears to be quite high in quartz content. The upper half is made of adobe mud bricks, most likely the work of local Native artisans, and is probably from the Inca period, with repairs being done when it was converted into a church.

Typical Inca style door blocked off with adobe bricks

In the photo above you can see that some of the stone blocks are damaged, and this apparently was done by heat as future pictures of the structure will show. Whether the heat was the result of local fires inside or outside of the church will be discussed as me move along.

More possible fire or heat damage

The darkening, cracks and pulverized areas of stone again are consistent with heat damage and this is near the top part of the stone wall section so the idea that it was caused by a local fire is highly unlikely. The most heavily damaged of the structure is in fact the east side, which is consistent with other heat effected structures of a megalithic nature that we have explored in Peru, Bolivia and even in Egypt; pointing to a possible global cataclysm from 12,000 years ago.

Trapezoidal niche on the north side with little damage

In the above photo we can see that there is little damage to the wall and niches of the north side, but closer examination reveals some discoloration apparently coming from the east.

Massive surface damage on the eastern wall

The most damaged area of the structure can be seen in the above photo. The right side of the eastern wall appears to have been the hardest hit by heat and the upper adobe section is not damaged at all, so the idea that there was a fire inside the church, which some claim from an event 100 or 200 years ago makes no sense what so ever. In the left side of the picture we see little damage and thus the epicenter of the destruction was on the right corner. Also, most ancient buildings were built with an orientation of more or less perfect north, south, east and west while the rectangular stone building of Huaytara is about 20

Me with the most damaged area at Huaytara

degrees off of that. Not an error as regards construction, but more likely that the orientation of the earth's axis was different when the building was initially built. This is consistent with the theory that the planet was struck by many catastrophic events 12,000 years ago at the end of the last ice age and is discussed in my book Aftershock.

Interior of the church at Huaytara

We next go inside the church to check out details of the internal construction. As you can see in the photo above there are darkened surfaces and flaking stone on the interior of the northern wall. This could very well be from a fire from the reasonably recent past, but the farther we move to the east, the greater the damage becomes. Thus, both recent fires and also an ancient cataclysm may have affected the inside walls of the structure over the course of its existence.

Unique angled indent trapezoid shapes at Huaytara

Standard "Inca style" trapezoid inside the church

32

The rather dubious road to Vilcashuaman

Vilcashuaman is an important llaca (city) Inca, built on the capital of its mythical rivals, the Chanca Confederation. Built in the times of the Incas Tupac Yupanqui and Huayna Capac (1400 to 1500 AD), it was one of the most important administrative centers of Tawantinsuyu, the Inca world. As head of the province, it housed up to 30,000 men as a garrison. The great wealth that contained its deposits, the beauty of its architecture and its strategic location on the route of the Capac Ñan (royal Inca road) aroused the interest of the Spanish conquerors (1532) who heard of its existence from the first moments of its arrival to Peruvian lands.

It is located in the district of the same name, Cangallo province 80 kilometers south east of the city of Ayacucho, department of Ayacucho, in southern Peru, on the left bank of the Pampas River at 3150 meters above sea level . The history of the foundation of this llacta begins at the beginning of the 15th century, with the triumph of the Inca Pachacutec over the hardened Chancas on the very doors of Cusco. A difficult victory that, had it been defeat, would have forever buried any Inca aspiration to form an empire.

View of the main Vilcashuaman complex

Pachacutec, in front of a powerful army, leaves the city of Cusco to start a campaign of conquests in the region of Ayacucho and Andahuaylas, the homeland of the Chancas. Crossing the Apurimac River and began its march dominating the Soras and Rucanas, imposing the latter, as a tribute, be the loaders of the litter in which the Inca and the nobility traveled. He sent Pachacutec to Apo Conde Mayta with part of the army to the region of Vilcas, who, after strong fights and opposing fierce resistance in hills and pucaras (fortresses) were finally subdued.

Rebuilt walls and niches at the Temple of the Sun

Located south of the trapezoidal square, the Temple of the Sun was built on a set of terraced terraces. Originally it had 2 trapezoidal spans, which were reached through stairways. On the second terrace you can still see some niches and trapezoidal niches, which is characterized by having inputs and outputs as buttresses. Next to the Temple of the Sun is the Acllawasi (House of the Chosen Women), the Temple of the Moon and other buildings, possibly occupied by priests and other people in charge of organizing and maintaining the cult of the Sun God. On the walls of this temple, after the Spanish conquest it was built the church of San Juan Bautista. This Church used the walls and contiguous

Likely pre-Inca megalithic stairs

environments as part of the Catholic temple, as it happened in other places, such as the Coricancha in Cusco and Huaytara, which we have just explored.

One side of the Ushnu

Located on the west side of the square, is another location called the Ushnu; a pyramid-shaped, terraced structure that was used by the Incas to preside at the most important ceremonies of the Tawantinsuyu. It is the largest, compared to the other Ushnu distributed on the main llaves of the Tawantinsuyu. Its structure is that of a rectangular pyramid formed by five platforms, accessing the highest part by a stairway, all built of stone. At the top there is to this day a double armchair carved in stone, which according to local tradition was covered with gold plates and was the place where the Inca and Coya (his wife) sat to impart justice and preside over ceremonies and rituals that took place in the plaza. Behind this structure there is another construction that is considered as the palace of Pachacutec. It is rectangular with three trapezoidal jamb doors built with great quality in its architecture, which is why it is attributed the greatest importance among the Inca buildings in the region.

Odd weathering in a wall at the Temple of the Sun

Like at Huaytara and other locations occupied by the Inca, Vilcashuaman is clearly megalithic and thus another very ancient site that the Inca found and reconstructed as the following photos will clearly show. Upon our recent visit in May 2018 we were told by local people that all of the basalt stone making up the megalithic parts of the structures were extracted and brought from a quarry 6 kilometers away, located on the top of a mountain.

Orientation of the Temple of the Sun/church

The above photo shows that the orientation of the main temple, now church at Vilcashuaman is about 30 degrees off where it should be, and again, it is likely that the earth's axis was different when it was constructed; not an error by the builders.

Inca reconstruction on the left and original on the right

The above photo shows that the Inca found what they would name the Temple of the Sun and rebuilt it largely from stones that they found in the location, which is obvious in the photo above. Unlike the tight fitting and mortar free joints on the right side of the above photo the Inca had to fill in their reconstruction efforts with broken pieces of stone, either fragments from the broken original wall or other rocks and debris that they found on the ground at the site or nearby.

Irene showing us melted surfaces at Huaytara

There is also clear evidence that the now church wall was hit by intense heat like what we saw at Huaytara; except perhaps more obvious. Different types of stone react to intense heat in different ways depending upon mineral content and density. As we saw at Huaytara the affected stone basically had its surfaces cracked and blown off, while at Vilcashuaman the stone shows signs of actual surface melting as well as cracking and breaking. The temperature required to melt such stone to the point where they literally become fused together is likely in excess of 2000 degrees centigrade, and that would not be from a standard local fire. The next photo shows in greater detail the melted surfaces and fusion of the stones. Again, likely the result of the cataclysmic events of 12,000 years ago as seen in the highlands of Peru as well as other locations in Egypt, such as Tanis and Karnak.

Melted basalt surface

More scorching seen above

Irene and large megalithic block

43

Damaged entry gate at the Ushnu

Main section of the Ushnu

We next move on to the Ushnu area of Vilcashuaman which is about a 5 minute walk from the Temple of the Sun/church area. We will see in the following photos that the Ushnu was also heavily damaged by cataclysmic events and was largely rebuilt by the Inca. The doorway in the above photos was open when we were there about 5 years ago but has had to be closed due to the chance that the lintel, which is broken in 2 could further deteriorate and hurt visitors. Again, such damage was not something done by the Spanish but had to have been the result of cataclysmic events. The Inca likely, upon arrival to the location reconstructed the structures as best as they could and used wood to reinforce the underside of the lintel which over the course of time would have to be replaced, and the Spanish apparently never used this structure.

Another Ushnu entrance

Almost perfect megalithic joint

Inca reconstruction

Trapezoid door with cataclysmic damage

Another trapezoid opening with major damage

Inca stone work

As a final look at the Ushnu area we see above carving into stone by the Inca of ceremonial symbols, possibly used in their divination practices. The etching marks are somewhat crude, and nothing like the refinement of the megalithic works of the much older master builders. This evidence by itself tells us that there were two distinct cultures in the area prior to the arrival of the Spanish, who had knowledge of concrete and clearly used that in the building of their church at Vilcashuaman.

We now move on to the last location covered in this book, that of the site of Wari, also located near to Ayacucho. This was the capital of the Wari culture that preceded the Inca, who collapsed around 1000 AD as the result of localized climate change. The Inca filled in the void that they left behind.

Massive 10 to 20 ton slab at Wari

In 1550, the chronicler Pedro Cieza de Leon recounted the discovery of several monumental structures approximately 25 km (15 miles) from the city of Huamanga, whose architecture differed from previously discovered Inca structures. He was describing Wari, the capital of the first Pan-Andean state, from the pre-Inca period (between 600 and 1000 A.D.).

Wari is an example of urban planning using pre-Hispanic engineering techniques. The urban core, which spanned some 400 hectares and at its peak was home to some 40,000 inhabitants, was strategically located in a

49

position with rapid access to the coast and the inland jungle, mid-way between the northern and southern mountain ranges, where they established administrative centers and colonies.

To visit Wari is to explore the Cheqowasi area, consisting of multi-level underground chambers with rectangular, circular, and quadrangular mezzanines, which were possibly mausoleums for rulers and nobles. The Moradochayoq area reveals evidence of close contact with the Tiawanaku, a contemporary culture located 1500 km (932 miles) from the Wari, in the giant Lake Titicaca basin.

Another massive slab at Wari

Just by looking at the 2 photos above, you can see that someone was at Wari before the actual Wari people. The 2 slabs shown so far were both found via recent excavations, and had to be dug out; whether the Wari in fact ever knew they were there is unknown, but quite likely. The stone itself appears to be basalt, and the quarry is several kilometers away; tough to move in this very mountainous and undulating landscape.

Large stones in the foreground with smaller ones behind

Basalt plumbing parts?

More of the presumed plumbing and aqueduct parts

Perhaps even more intriguing and mysterious are the stones in the above photo, some with almost perfectly circular holes bored through the center. Once again this is basalt, which could not have been shaped by the Wari as they barely were of a bronze age level of technology and their source of bronze may have been from the Tiwanaku culture whose center was 1500 kilometers away. As stated above, though with question marks, it would appear that these along with many others, some damaged and in fact broken into 2 or more pieces were components of a plumbing system.

When we visiting the site previously all of these stones were in another location nearby, and were covered in weeds. Whether they were originally found there during the recent excavations is unknown.

Large stone slabs at Cheqowasi

More large slabs at Cheqowasi

Smart phone app shows perfectly level

The so called tombs seen in the above 2 photos, which could have been used by the Wari but did not make them appear to be perfectly horizontally and vertically level and this indicates that they are in their original locations. The contrast between them and the Wari surrounding walls is quite obvious, and the former yet again seem to have been damaged by a cataclysmic event or series of events.

What the original function of these containers or vessels was is unknown, but perhaps they were water containers and are contemporary with the plumbing parts seen in earlier photos. A major cataclysm would have destroyed their usefulness and thus would have been abandoned and it is possible that the original builders also perished at this time.

The author on top of the mysterious container

The author inside

Holes inside the container

56

More large basalt slabs

More megalithic evidence

Even more massive slabs at Wari

View of the Andes mountain called Chicon

Remains of an Inca period wall; notice trapezoid niches

We now move into the Sacred Valley of Peru and are at Chicon, the name of the snowcapped mountain in the background, the stream that runs through this location and the village close by. We were alerted by an American living in the village, via cell phone that he had found an ancient structure that had large stones locked together in a series of walls and since we had never heard of the place we had to go.

Our friend Willko, an Indigenous wisdom keeper from Cusco decided to join us because he had never heard of the place either, so we hired a taxi for the 1 and a half hour drive into the Sacred Valley and tried to phone our contact when we were in the general area which proved successful. It cannot be stressed too much that the number of ancient Inca and pre-Inca sites in the Sacred which still exist in whole or in part is incredibly vast.

Polygonal pre-Inca stone work with Inca adobe above

Pre-Inca below and Inca above

Some may think that the adobe is a Spanish colonial addition, but since their basic opinion about the Inca and other native people was one of distaste, following the flow of the trapezoid shape is highly unlikely.

Willko at a solar alignment temple

As we were already in the Sacred Valley we decided to explore another ancient site that Willko knew of, about a one hour drive south on the highway which was built directly on top of an Inca road. It is quite odd for an Inca structure, which tend to be rectangular in shape but its original function made complete sense when we deduced that it was a temple built to track solar alignment. There are only 2 windows that penetrate the interior from outside; one for the winter solstice and the other for the summer solstice. A 100 percent Inca structure with no signs of megalithic foundation, but intriguing none the less.

Interior of the solar alignment temple

Also located at this site are Inca period terraces, as the climate is so mild that crops can be grown 12 months of the year in the Sacred Valley and in fact the Ministry of Culture of Peru has begun programs to rebuild some of the larger terracing systems called andene in the Inca language. This is partially to increase the number of ancient locations for tourists, both foreign and domestic to visit, and also curiously to replant on them in order to understand why the Inca forms and techniques of agriculture were so astonishingly successful.

Behind the solar temple are rather crude Inca buildings of mainly adobe construction, but there is also a huge boulder, likely having rolled from a much higher elevation that has a snake carved into the surface, making a fountain. Though I had seen photos of it before, this was my first actual glimpse of it.

As we headed back north in the Sacred Valley and drove back to Cusco we passed one of the largest terracing and food storage areas of the Inca world, called Machu Colca, which means the ancient storage place.

Machu Colca

The next place to explore is known by few, and took more than 2 years to locate after a German guy had sent me 2 black and white photos. I emailed him back and asked for the location, and his short and simple answer was "go find it." Though now on local tourist maps it is located in a side valley branching off from the

Sacred Valley and the rough dirt road that gets you close to it is an Inca road that leads to Cusco. Who made it, when and how is as yet unknown but it was clearly used by the Inca for ceremonial purposes. Known locally as Naupa Iglesia, where Naupa is Inca for "ancient" or for the "ancient ones" while iglesia is Spanish for church.

Three niches in a stone outcrop

The "portal" in bedrock in the cave

The ascent of at least a few hundred stairs is required to reach the cave and monuments of Naupa Huaca. The staircase itself was likely made by the Inca, but the monuments are made of very hard volcanic stone and thus were likely the work of a much older culture that had some form of high technology.

Inca construction in the cave

Contrast the work above with the previous photos and you can clearly see that they are not the work of the same artisans. The trapezoid shapes are an indication of Inca construction, adopted from the much older megalithic structures, and the use of rough stone and adobe is also how a high percentage of Inca buildings were made.

The presence of terraces on both sides of the long staircase below the cave could very well indicate that people lived in the cave, likely Inca priests, and had their own food supply. Not exactly in the middle of nowhere, as the huge Inca complex of Ollantaytambo is about 12 kilometers away, the setting of Naupa Huaca has the feel of a place of solitary or small group contemplation.

Megalithic granite blocks at Ollantaytambo

Ollantaytambo (Quechua: Ullantaytampu) is a town and an Inca archaeological site in southern Peru some 72 km (45 mi) by road northwest of the city of Cusco. It is located at an altitude of 2,792 m (9,160 ft) above sea level in the district of Ollantaytambo, province of Urubamba, Cusco region. During the Inca Empire, Ollantaytambo was the royal estate of Emperor Pachacutec, who conquered the region, and built the town and a ceremonial center. At the time of the Spanish conquest of Peru, it served as a stronghold for Manco Inca Yupanqui, leader of the Inca resistance. Nowadays, located in what is called the Sacred Valley of the Incas, it is an important tourist attraction on account of its Inca ruins and its location en route to one of the most common starting points for the four-day, three-night hike known as the Inca Trail.

Around the mid-15th century, the Inca emperor Pachacutec conquered and razed Ollantaytambo; the town and the nearby region were incorporated into his personal estate. The emperor rebuilt the town with sumptuous constructions and undertook extensive works of terracing and irrigation in the Urubamba Valley; the town provided lodging for the Inca nobility, while the terraces were farmed by yanakuna, retainers of the emperor. After Pachacutec's death, the estate came under the administration of his panaqa, his family clan.

Massive terraces at Ollantaytambo

During the Spanish conquest of Peru, Ollantaytambo served as a temporary capital for Manco Inca, leader of the native resistance against the conquistadors. He fortified the town and its approaches in the direction of the former Inca capital of Cusco, which had fallen under Spanish domination. In 1536, on the plain of Mascabamba, near Ollantaytambo, Manco Inca defeated a Spanish expedition, blocking their advance from a set of high terraces and flooding the plain. Despite his victory, however, Manco Inca did not consider his position tenable, so the following year, he withdrew to the heavily forested site of Vilcabamba, where he established the Neo-Inca State.

Megalithic wall on the left and Inca work on the right

In the above photo you can see great differences in the forms of construction; exquisite polygonal granite work on the left and much rougher on the right. This indicates that Ollantaytambo was a very old megalithic site that the Inca discovered a rebuilt, as was Cusco, Machu Pic'chu etc. Also, the stone on the right is a mix of relatively smaller rocks reasonably well fitted together while the stonework on the left is for all purposes perfect. Also, the stone on the left is from a quarry located on top of a mountain on the other side of the sacred Valley at a site called Cachiccata, and those on the right are a mix of local and brought in stones.

Inca reconstruction

Massive granite slab on a poor foundation

Another Inca repair

Clearly the last 3 photos show you that the Inca found Ollantaytambo in a state of disrepair and the victim of some ki[...] repaired

Probable machine marks

Broken pieces of granite from the older constructions and loca[...] slate like stone were used to make terraces, stairs and buildings, usually cemented together with local clay as mortar. Compared to other sights where the megalithic aspects usually form the foundation of later Inca work, at Ollantaytambo the megalithic is mainly on top of the hill, and called the Sun Temple.

Megalithic blocks in a river near the Sun Temple

Academics claim that the Sun Temple was never completed by the Inca for some mysterious reason, but it is quite clear that cataclysmic activity caused the east and west sides to collapse and fall to the ground below. The Inca as said then recycled the broken stones. One dead giveaway is that the staircase leading up to the Sun Temple is very irregular and uneven, whereas what remains of the Sun Temple is close to being technically perfect.

Machu Pic'chu is said to have been built around 1450 to 1460. Its construction appears to date to the period of the two great Inca rulers, Pachacutec Inca Yupanqui

(1438 to 71) and Tupac Inca Yupanqui (1472 to 93). There is a consensus among archaeologists that Pachacutec ordered the construction of the royal estate for himself, most likely after his successful military campaign. Though Machu Pic'chu is considered to be a "royal" estate, surprisingly, the estate would not have been passed down in the line of succession. It was only used for approximately 80 years before being abandoned seemingly due to destruction of the Spanish Conquests in other parts of the Inca Empire. It is possible that most of its inhabitants died from smallpox introduced by travelers before the Spanish conquistadors arrived in the area or that the Inca abandoned it in order that the Spanish never find it.

View of a portion of Machu Pic'chu

Megalithic Sun Temple left and front; poor wall on the right

During its use as a royal estate, it is estimated that no more than 750 people lived there at a time, most people being support staff.

Fine construction in the foreground and right side

(yanaconas, yana) who lived there permanently. Though the estate belonged to Pachacutec, religious specialists and temporary specialized workers (mayocs) lived there as well, most likely for the ruler's well-being and enjoyment. During the harsher season, staff dropped down to around a hundred servants and a few religious specialists focused only on maintenance.

Megalithic wall showing separation damage

Studies show that according to their skeletal remains, most people who lived there were immigrants from diverse backgrounds. They lacked the chemical markers and osteological markers they would have if they had been living there their whole lives. Instead, there was bone damage from various species of water parasites indigenous to different areas of Peru. There were also varying osteological stressors and varying chemical densities suggesting varying long term diets characteristic of specific regions that were spaced apart. These diets are composed of varying levels of maize, potatoes, grains, legumes, and fish, but the overall most recent short-term diet for these people composed of less fish and more corn. This suggests that several of the immigrants were from more coastal areas and moved to Machu Pic'chu where corn was a larger portion of food intake. The skeletal remains found at Machu Picchu are also unique in their level of natural bone damage from laborious activities.

Inca repair on top of older megalithic

Most people found at the site had lower levels of arthritis and bone fractures found in most sites of the Inca Empire.

Inca above and megalithic below

Inca individuals that have arthritis and bone fractures are typically those who performed heavy physical labor (such as the Mit'a) and/or served in the Inca military.
Like at Ollantaytambo, the above photos of Machu Pic'chu clearly indicate that 2 distinct cultures were involved in its construction.

View of some terraces and the Machu Pic'chu quarry

Rather than being something constructed over the course of 2 or so decades, it is more likely that Machu Pic'chu was created over centuries after the megalithic core was first discovered in the high jungle.

The author wondering in amazement

Astonishing megalithic wall

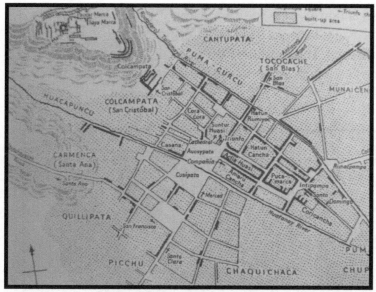
Early topographical map of Cusco

The above map was made soon after the Spanish took hold of Cusco in about 1533 AD. What is most intriguing about it are the presence of thick walls and thinner ones which actually distinguish the wider megalithic structures in the city as compared to the thinner Inca ones. This by itself is evidence that the Inca discovered an abandoned megalithic city around 1000 years ago and decided to make it their capital, after fleeing warfare and drought at Lake Titicaca to the south.

Cusco, more properly written as Qosqo means "navel" or "center" in the Inca language, commonly called Quechua but more properly Runa Simi (peoples' language) and Cusco remained the geographic and cultural center from its Inca discovery until the destruction by the Spanish. A more logical location for their capital would have been in the Sacred Valley due to the high and local food production, but the Inca were very likely impressed by the ruins they found and thus named it Qosqo.

Megalithic wall with Inca repair on top

Known and explored by few above Cusco and close to the massive megalithic walls of Saqsaywaman lies a site, which is in fact part of the Saqsaywaman complex known locally as Zone X. It is a series of walls that were found and repaired by the Inca, as well as about 20 tunnels which appear to be natural in formation but were later widened and smoothed out.

As the stone here is metamorphosed limestone it is unlikely that the Inca bronze tools could have shaped the tunnels and thus could very well have been executed by the megalithic builders for reasons as yet unknown.

Megalithic wall section

Strange cut out in the bedrock

Saqsaywaman in the background

More strange cut outs

Even more strange cut outs

And more

More cut out shapes at Qenqo

In Quechua, Qenqo means labyrinth or zig-zag and the temple is named for the crooked canal cut out of its rock. Although it is clear the canal carried some sort of liquid, researchers have been forced to guess at its purpose, and at what liquid it transported. Hypotheses range from carrying holy water, chicha (corn beer), or blood. All three indicate that Qenqo was used for death rituals, possibly to embalm bodies or detect whether a person lived a good life by the course the liquid followed.

Qenqo is a unique temple in its construction as well, having been entirely carved out of a gigantic monolith. Stretched across a hillside, the temple is carved out of rock and marries the man-made tunnels with natural chambers. One of these chambers features 19 small niches and is set up as an amphitheater. Once again, the purpose of the theater has been lost over time, but most agree the area was used for some type of sacrifice to the sun, moon and star gods who were worshipped at the site. There is little evidence that the Inca ever performed human sacrifice.

Inside the Qenqo labyrinth

Huge stones at Little Qenqo

Megalithic with Inca repair

Interesting curved shaping

More cut outs in bedrock

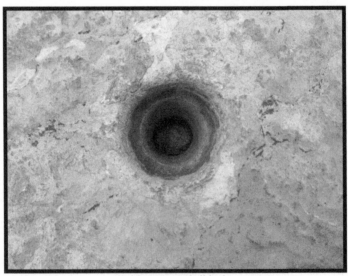

Odd ancient drill hole

Massive Chinkana (tunnel) at Saqsaywman

Back side of the Chinkana formation

93

A full description of the main Saqsaywaman site can be read about in my earlier book Lost Ancient Technology of Peru and Bolivia. Our final destination is Tiwanaku and Puma Punku in Bolivia.

Famous H blocks at Puma Punku

Pumapunku or Puma Punku (Aymara and Quechua puma cougar, puma, punku door, Hispanicized Puma Puncu) is part of a large temple complex or monument group that is part of the Tiwanaku Site near Tiwanaku, in western Bolivia. It is believed to date to AD 536 and later.

Tiwanaku is significant in Inca traditions because it is believed to be the site where the world was created. In

Aymara, Puma Punku's name means "The Door of the Puma". The Pumapunku complex consists of an unwalled western court, a central unwalled esplanade, a terraced platform mound that is faced with stone, and a walled eastern court.

The Pumapunku is a terraced earthen mound that is faced with blocks. It is 167.36 metres (549.1 feet) wide along its north–south axis and 116.7 metres (383 feet) long along its east–west axis. On the northeast and southeast corners of the Pumapunku, it has 20-metre (66-foot) wide projections that extend 27.6 metres (91 feet) north and south from the rectangular mound.

Massive andesite slab at Tiwanaku

The eastern edge of the Pumapunku is occupied by what is called the

Plataforma Lítica. This structure consists of a stone terrace that is 6.75 by 38.72 metres (22.1 by 127.0 feet) in dimension. This terrace is paved with multiple enormous stone blocks. It contains the largest stone slab found in both the Pumapunku and Tiwanaku Site, measuring 7.81 metres (25.6 feet) long, 5.17 metres (17.0 feet) wide and averages 1.07 m (3 ft 6 in) thick. Based upon the specific gravity of the red sandstone from which it was carved, this stone slab has been estimated to weigh 131 metric tons.

The other stonework and facing of the Pumapunku consists of a mixture of andesite and red sandstone.

Catastrophic destruction at Puma Punku

Pumapunku's core consists of clay, while the fill underlying selected parts of its edge consists of river sand and cobbles instead of clay. Excavations have documented "three major building epochs, in addition to small repairs and remodeling".

Massive andesite blocks at Tiwanaku

At its peak, Pumapunku is thought to have been "unimaginably wondrous," adorned with polished metal plaques, brightly colored ceramic and fabric ornamentation, and visited by costumed citizens, elaborately dressed priests, and elites decked in exotic jewelry. Current understanding of this complex is limited due to its age, the lack of a written record, and the current deteriorated state of the structures due to treasure hunting, looting, stone mining for building stone and railroad ballast, and natural weathering.

The author with an andesite block

The area within the kilometer separating the Pumapunku and Kalasasaya complexes has been surveyed using ground-penetrating radar, magnetometry, induced electrical conductivity, and magnetic susceptibility. The geophysical data collected from these surveys and excavations have revealed the presence of numerous man-made structures in the area between the Pumapunku and Kalasasaya complexes. These structures include the wall foundations of buildings and compounds, water conduits, pool-like features, revetments, terraces, residential compounds, and widespread gravel pavements, all of which now lie buried and hidden beneath the modern ground's surface.

Sense of scale

Megalithic staircase at Puma Punku; ancient port?

Piles of stone and Spanish colonial grinding wheel unfinished

The famous Sun Gate of Tiwanaku

Irene and engineer Tony inspecting flat surfaces

Engineer Tony measuring magnetic anomalies

More drill holes and seemingly machined channels

Clearly the conventional statements as regards the history of Puma Punku and Tiwanaku are very inaccurate, to say the least. The fact that many of the large stones were found buried underground at least hints that a cataclysm struck the area, and quite probably the same as we have seen at other megalithic locations in this book. Also, at the time that academics insist that the major construction took place, as in the 6th century AD, the local Tiwanaku people were barely in the bronze age.

The photos you have seen above indicate very strongly that an advanced civilization built both Tiwanaku and Puma Punku, which were in the ancient past the same location. Cataclysmic events may have then destroyed the culture or made them flee, leaving nothing but the damaged megalithic remains for us to study today

Magnetic anomalies, precision hard stone cutting and the smelting of bronze at 13,000 feet above sea level are just a few of the facts that do not fit into the standard academic story and that is why it is one of my favourite locations. I will in future write a book solely as regards the magnetic oddities and advanced machining that we see here. Also taking into account that all of the original work was done in red sandstone from a quarry 15 kilometers away and grey andesite from a separate quarry some 75 kilometers in the distance on top of a volcano adds to the mystery and fascination of this place.

This concludes volume 2 of the Lost Ancient Technology Of Peru series and whether there will be a volume 3 or even 4 is unknown as I have explored most of the ancient locations in Peru and Bolivia that are known to academics and local people. It would be arrogant to say that I have seen them all, and I hope that others are hiding in the high jungle areas yet to be discovered, or perhaps even in the shallow areas of Lake Titicaca.

I do hope that you have gleaned from the mounting and frankly quite obvious evidence that at least one and possibly more advanced technological civilizations existed in Peru and Bolivia long before most academics will admit, and prior to the famous cultures such as the Inca and Tiwanaku people.

Made in the USA
Las Vegas, NV
03 April 2021